£ 1·35

Published in Great Britain by
World Distributors (Manchester) Limited.
A Member of the Pentos Group,
P.O. Box 111, 12 Lever Street, Manchester M60 1TS
Printed in Italy.
SBN 7235 0455 5

ROD STEWART ANNUAL 1978

CONTENTS

Written by Ann Tucek

Designed by Peter Corri

ROD the mod to STEWART the superstar

Few musicians can claim to have played a major role in the development of rock music as we know it today, let alone claim to have attained the status of rock superstar. However, Rod Stewart is one such phenomenon.

He began to carve his career at the start of the Beatles era in the early sixties, when he sang and played harmonica with Jimmy Powell's Five Dimensions, and by the time the sixties rolled into the seventies, Rod had become a major name on the British rock scene with the Faces.

It was the release of a solo album, *Every Picture Tells A Story* and the accompanying single *Maggie May* in 1971, however, which took Rod the Mod into the Superstar league. The single and album topped their respective British and American charts in the same week!

In this annual we take a look at Rod's career, to find out the background to his success, as well as looking at his time with the Faces, his stage act, his love of football and, not least, his music!

the ROD STEWART File

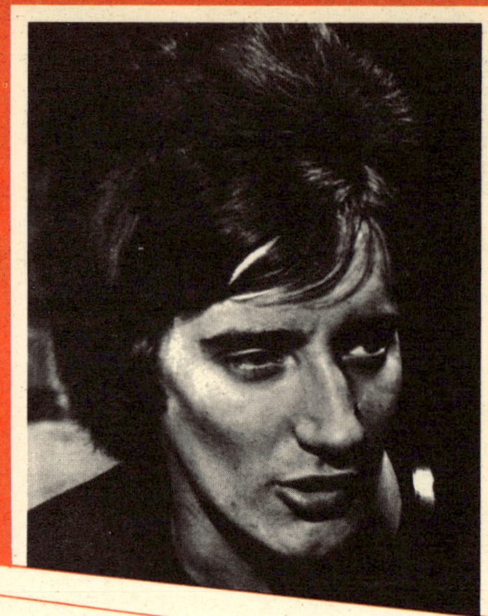

From Rod the Mod in 1963 (top left) to Stewart the Superstar in 1976 (bottom right).

NAME: Roderick David Stewart

DATE OF BIRTH: January 10, 1945

PLACE OF BIRTH: Highgate, North London

PARENTS: Robert and Elsie Stewart, who ran a newsagent's in Archway

FIRST SINGLE: *Good Morning Little School Girl* (October 1964)

FIRST SOLO ALBUM: *An Old Raincoat Will Never Let You Down*

FIRST TV APPEARANCES: *Beat Room* (BBC2); *Late Date* (Southern); *Ready Steady Go*—all 1964. *Rod The Mod* documentary (ITV)—November 1965

GROUPS: Jimmy Powell and the Five Dimensions (September 1963–January 1964), The Hoochie Coochie Men (January 1964–April 1965), Steampacket (April 1965–October 1966), Shotgun Express (October 1966–December 1966), The Jeff Beck Group (October 1966–October 1969), The Small Faces (October 1969–February 1970), The Faces (February 1970–December 1975), The Rod Stewart Group (October 30, 1976–)

FIRST LONG-TERM RECORDING CONTRACT: Mercury Records (with Lou Reizner as producer) in October 1968

OTHER RECORD LABELS FOR SOLO RECORDINGS: Decca, Columbia, Immediate, Mercury, Warner Brothers and Riva

the Rod Stewart story

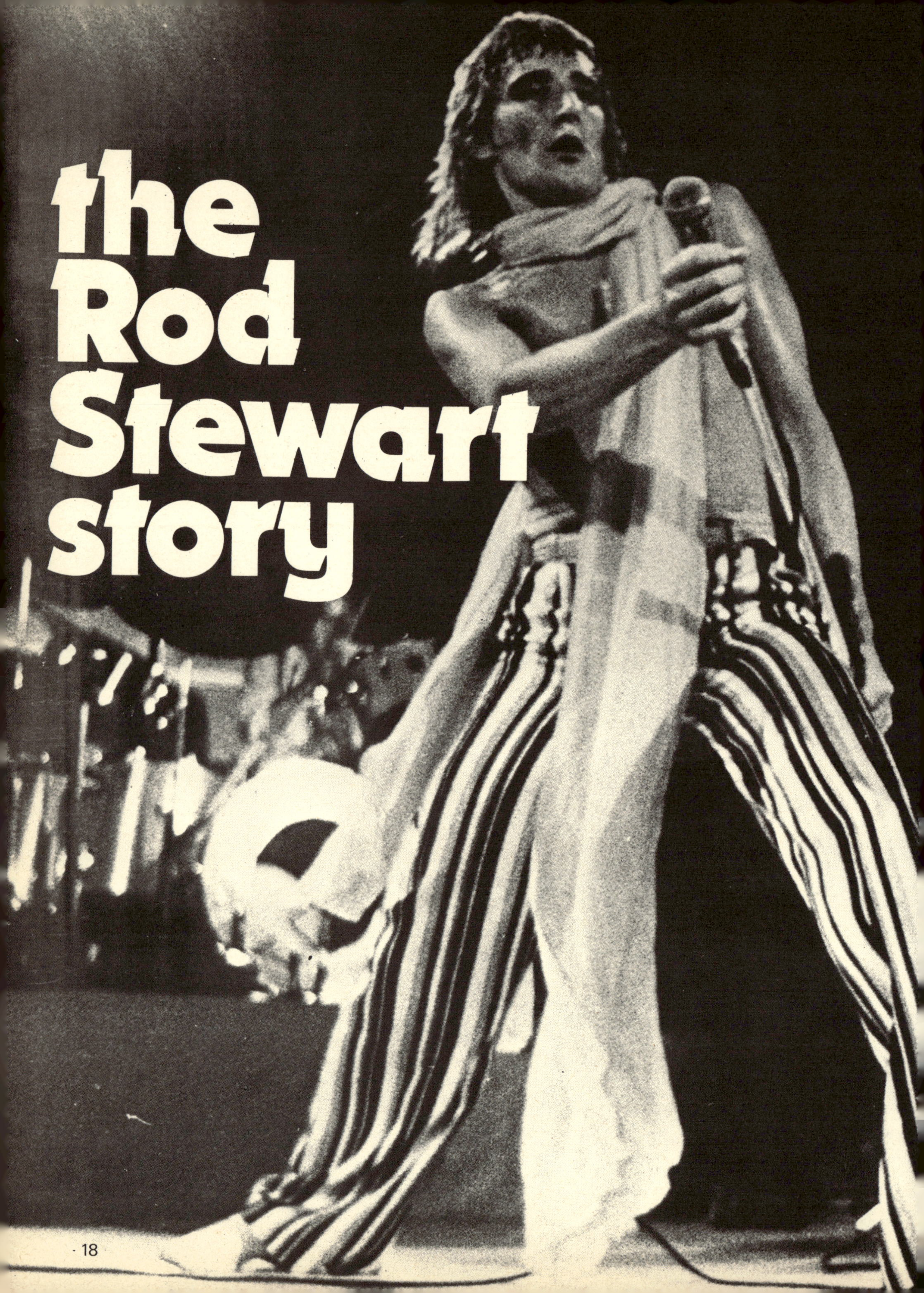

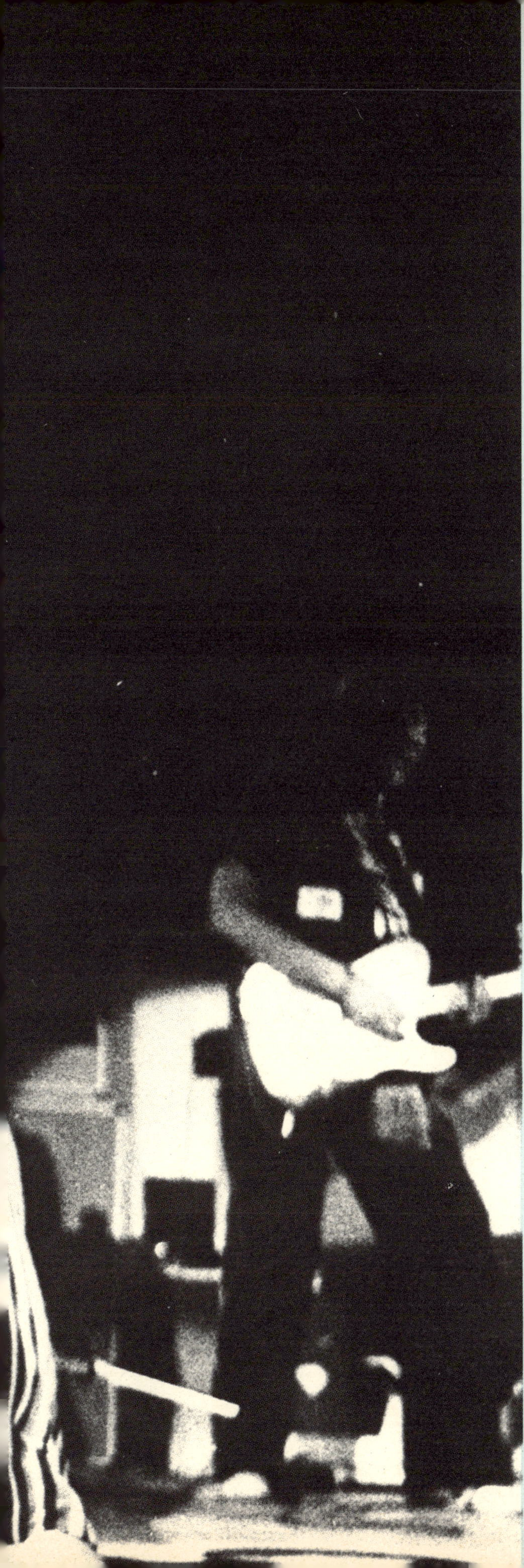

Roderick David Stewart was born at Highgate, North London, on January 10th 1945, the son of Robert and Elsie Stewart. Rod's father ran a newsagent's in Archway, and he often helped out in the shop, selling the newspapers he was one day destined to be making the news in himself. And now, in less than a decade, Rod has made the transition from little known 'Mod' of the sixties to the flamboyant and glamorous rock Superstar of the seventies.

Rod's natural charm and personality have long made him the target of attractive models and film stars, and perhaps only Liz Taylor's and Richard Burton's romances and marriages have filled more newspapers and magazines with stories and photographs than Rod and his girlfriends. That was before Mr Stewart's much publicised romance with Britt Ekland started selling papers for newsagents up and down the country, however.

To find out more about the making of a Superstar, we must first go back to number 507 Archway Road, where Rod was born. He was the youngest of Mr and Mrs Stewart's five children—the others were sisters Mary and Peggy and brothers Don and Bob. Rod's father had moved down to London from Scotland when he was only sixteen, to take up an apprenticeship as a plumber, and there he met Rod's mother, who came from Upper Holloway.

One of young Rod's first loves was football, as he says: "One of my earliest memories is of the pictures my brothers had on their bedroom wall. They were of Scottish footballers."

This, together with his father's Scottish birth, helped Rod to develop his fierce Scottish pride alongside his love of soccer. At the same time, the

parties which were frequently held at Rod's home were also his first contact with music and his never-lost love of Al Jolson.

"I can remember the words of lots of old songs because of those parties. We might not have been a musical family, but everybody would have a go. My brother Don is a natural entertainer and the finest Al Jolson impersonator I've ever seen. Mind you, I was very small then, and too young to really appreciate those nights."

School saw Rod attending the Highgate Primary, where he failed his eleven plus, although he felt certain he had passed, and then the William Grimshaw Secondary Modern School.

Rod showed more distinction in sport, however, and went on to captain

Left and below: Rod in 1963.

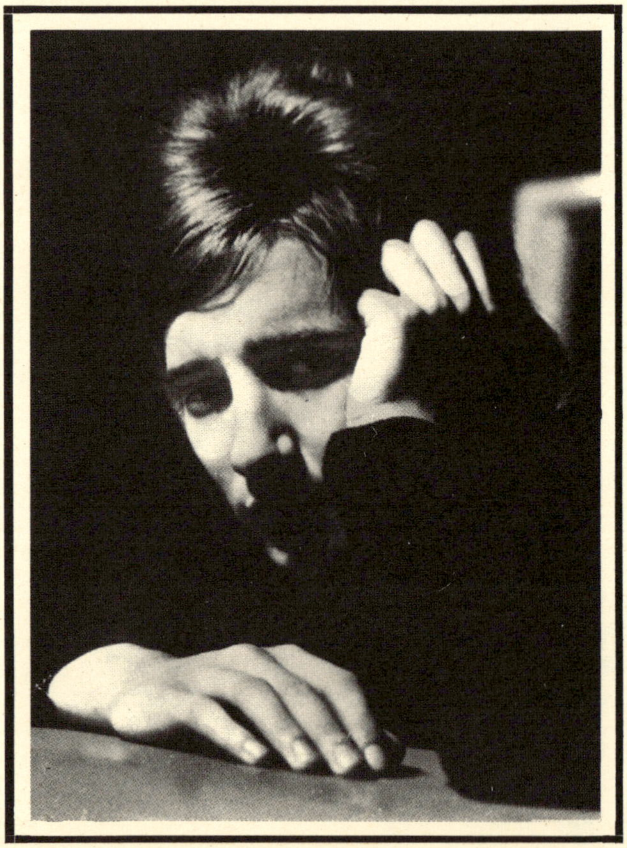

Rod (left), Long John Baldry, Julie Driscoll and Brian Auger, who formed Steampacket.

both the soccer and cricket teams. But a black spot on his school record occurred when he was dismissed as a prefect for letting off a fire extinguisher. It was while he was at this secondary school that Rod's father bought him his first guitar, although at the time any thoughts of becoming a top rock star must have been well hidden.

In fact, Rod hated music at school, as his music teacher was always asking him to sing in front of the class, something he didn't enjoy at all at the time! When the time finally came to leave school Rod had still not started to think seriously about music, and he had no idea as to what to do about a career, so he went to work for a wallpaper manufacturer, making the silk screens the patterns were printed from.

"It was so boring. I was only working there for about nine months, but it seemed more like ten years!"

Rod's main interest at the time was still football and, having made the grade as an England schoolboy international, he served a three-month apprenticeship with Brentford. Gradually, however, Rod was now getting more and more interested in music—there were a lot of exciting things going on back in the early sixties—and he began to feel his real future was as a musician. Also Rod was experiencing a growing ambition to find fame.

"I knew I had to be famous at something, but it didn't matter what—medicine, jumping off the Eiffel Tower, anything . . . I just had to be famous."

Rod was seventeen when he abandoned his apprenticeship with Brentford and set off to hitch and busk round Europe. In St Tropez he was making 50 francs an hour playing, and sleeping on the beach. While he was in

France, Rod played for a time with Memphis Slim—who encouraged his love of the blues—until he was deported back home by the British Consul.

By the time Rod was nineteen, his vocal experience was still somewhat limited, but he could then play the harmonica and was asked to join Jimmy Powell's Five Dimensions.

Jimmy Powell's band was part of the growing British R & B scene at the time, supporting groups like the Rolling Stones. The association did not work out as Rod had hoped, however, for he was only allowed to sing backing vocals, but it was while Rod was with the Dimensions that a meeting took

place which was to prove a major turning point in his career.

The meeting was with the legendary white bluesman Long John Baldry, and it happened at Twickenham railway station.

"I had heard Rod before," Baldry recalls, "playing harmonica, but never singing. But there was Roddy, sitting on the platform waiting for a train and singing the blues. He rather impressed me, so I asked him how he would fancy a gig. That was how Rod joined my band as a vocalist."

Rod Stewart performed with Baldry's Hoochie Coochie Men, earning £35 a week, and singing numbers like *Night Time is the Right Time* and

Tiger in Your Tank. This was in 1964. He also recorded his first solo single, *Good Morning Little Schoolgirl* at this time, but then the Hoochie Coochie Men disbanded. Rod then performed for a while with a group known as the Soul Agents, until the formation of Steampacket in mid-1965.

This new outfit gave Stewart, Baldry, Julie Driscoll and Brian Auger equal billing on stage and was a music revue on the road in which each artist had their own slot, finally ending up on stage together. The group's music was moving away from the earlier R & B towards the American soul styles and this brought Steampacket to the attention of the growing British club audiences.

It was during this period that Rod began to absorb the major influences of the late Sam Cooke, as well as listening to people like Ramblin' Jack Elliott and Eddie Cochran, and thus began to develop his own distinctive folky blues style.

"I listened to everyone and picked up a bit from them all," Rod maintains. "I listened to Sam Cooke for about two years and I know I sounded a bit like him."

Rod also has one little-realised claim to fame at this time—he played harmonica on Millie's big international hit *My Boy Lollipop*, but one of his most significant recordings ever was *Shake* in 1966, backed by Brian Auger and heavily influenced by Sam Cooke's vocal style.

Rod and Britt—the newsman's ideal couple.

By the summer of 1966, however, there was a lot of friction in Steampacket, and Rod left to join Shotgun Express, singing alongside Beryl Marsden, with Peter Green (guitar), Peter Barden (keyboards), Dave Ambrose (bass), and Mick Fleetwood (drums).

Rod had built up a considerable reputation as a singer by the time he joined the Jeff Beck Group as a founder member and front man early in 1967, and it was then that he began his long-standing and fruitful association with Ron Wood. Stewart's contributions graced the group's two albums, *Truth* and *Beck-Ola* and he began to overcome his shyness on stage, gradually developing his spectacular stage act.

Left: Rod with Ron.
Below: The Faces after Tetsu had replaced Ronnie Lane.

As so often happens, however, a clash of personalities saw the demise of yet another band. In the October of 1969, Rod followed Ron Wood to join Ronnie Lane, Kenny Jones and Ian MacLagan in the re-formed (Small) Faces. Just after joining the Faces, Rod signed a solo recording contract with Mercury, firmly paving the way for his extraordinary dual success.

With the Faces, Rod made five albums and several successful singles including *Stay With Me* in 1972 and *Cindy Incidentally* in 1973. But they were essentially a live band, and a very exciting one at that. By the time Ronnie Lane left in mid-1973, however, the career of Rod Stewart, Superstar, was by far overshadowing the Faces.

Superstar is a term often loosely used, but this is not so in Rod's case. In fact, it is even easy to establish exactly when he made the transition from star to Superstar.

It happened on the release of his third solo album *Every Picture Tells a Story*. His first two albums, *An Old Raincoat Will Never Let You Down* and *Gasoline Alley*, had met with some success, but *Every Picture* stormed to the top of the charts on both sides of the Atlantic as did the single from it, *Maggie May*. Rod thus had the unique achievement of sitting at the top of both British and American singles and album charts in the same week.

Now, more than six years and a string of hits later, Rod is still at the top of the tree and if his well publicised romances ever fail to keep him in the public eye, we can be sure his music will still do it for him.

ROD'S SUPERCHARGED STAGESHOW

If you've been a Rod Stewart fan for any length of time, the chances are that you've been to a Faces or a Stewart concert, and know that there is nothing quite like it! It's not just that the songs are good—and they always are—that makes for a memorable experience. It's Rod himself!

Few rock stars can ever perform with such presence and charisma as Mr Stewart does. We all know he has immense talent, it's there to hear on all his records, but there is nothing quite like catching Super Rod live!

Long gone is the dirty raincoat Rod used to wear on stage with the Faces, however, as it wouldn't suit the superstar image, but the energy is still there—no one can do quite what Rod does when he holds the microphone stand up high in the air in between leaping about the stage, onto the piano in one bound, and off it again just as energetically.

When Rod sings his songs, many are known word for word by the audience, and they all want to clap hands and join in the singing—it's better than being at a party.

You can be sure Mr Stewart and his band are all enjoying themselves, and you can bet the fans are!

Rod with 'Faces' Ron Wood and Tetsu in 1974.

Rod at Olympia

In the week before Christmas 1976, Rod's first tour with his new band reached the climax of ten weeks touring Europe with gigs in Birmingham and at Olympia in London.

Needless to say, the tour was a sell-out, playing to packed houses at all the venues, and, for those fans lucky enough to be at any of the concerts, it was certainly an unforgettable experience. Our cameraman was at Olympia to capture the Stewart magic on film, and here are some of the pix. They will either bring back some great memories, or give you an idea of just what you missed!

THE FACES BEHIND

It was while Rod Stewart was with the Jeff Beck Group that he finally established a name for himself as the lead singer of a band, at the same time spreading his name in America, and, growing in confidence, he made his first solo album, *An Old Raincoat Will Never Let You Down*.

It was at that time that Steve Marriott had departed from the Small Faces, leaving them in disarray. Then, when Ron Wood left Jeff Beck to join the remaining Small Faces, it seemed to be a natural step for a newly established singer to take, too. So Rod decided to follow his friend and join the Faces. The other names behind the Faces—besides Ron Wood—were Kenny Jones, Ronnie Lane and Ian MacLagan. They helped to turn Rod from a comparative unknown into a national hero, so let's take a closer look at them.

The Small Faces, as they were originally called, were formed in 1965 by Steve Marriott (born January 30 1947), vocals and

The Small Faces, left to right: Steve Marriott, Ian MacLagan, Kenny Jones and Ronnie Lane.

THE FACES

guitar; Ronnie Lane (April 1 1946), bass; Jimmy Winston, organ, and Kenny Jones (September 16 1948), drums. They were very much *the* mod group. Ian MacLagan (May 12 1945) replaced Winston after the group's first hit single, *Watcha Gonna Do About It*.

The next single flopped, but the Small Faces were destined to become regular hitmakers, for *Hey Girl, All Or Nothing* and *My Mind's Eye* all reached the top ten, *All Or Nothing* making the top slot. These were all Lane/Marriott songs. More hits, like *Itchycoo Park* (1967) and *Lazy Sunday* (1968) followed, but the group's image remained the same.

After making the much-acclaimed album *Ogden's Nut Gone Flake* in 1968, however, it became obvious that the individual faces did not seem to be fitting within the group anymore, and Steve Marriott left to join Peter Frampton in Humble Pie.

The remaining three Small Faces started looking for a replacement guitarist and vocalist, and Ron Wood, who had been playing bass with Jeff Beck, jumped at the chance to play lead again. Rod and Ron had been friends and had played together since the founding of the Jeff Beck Group in 1967, and so a new vocalist arrived as the fifth face.

Another new face was to be Tetsu Yamauchi, who replaced Ronnie Lane when he left in 1973. The end of the Faces came in December 1975, with Rod's announcement that he was going to go solo, Woody by then having become virtually a permanent member of the Stones.

The Faces right to left: Rod, Ronnie Lane, Ron Wood, Kenny Jones and Ian MacLagan.

SOCCERING IT

Football is a serious business for Rod.

TO US?

Two of Rod's first loves were soccer and Scotland (it's difficult to say in which order)! Rod might have been born in London, but his Scottish parentage has made him just as fervent a fan of Scottish football as any Scot from north of the border.

Apart from shouting the praises of those players who wear the famous blue jerseys for international football whenever he gets the chance, Rod will go to almost any lengths to watch his two favourite teams—Scotland and Manchester United (they've had a long history of famous Scottish players, Denis Law was an early idol of Rod's, even before Tommy Docherty became manager).

Law in his United heyday.

Tommy Docherty, Rod's choice for Prime Minister.

As a boy, Rod was no mean footballer, either, playing on the wing for England Schoolboys (sorry Rod!), and he had a three-month trial for Brentford. As we know, soccer's loss was to be music's gain, but Rod never misses the chance for a game of football whenever he can.

It is interesting to note that one of Rod's closest friends now is Denis Law, the player he idolised for years when he was with Manchester United—but what does Rod think of Tommy Docherty?

"I would like Tommy Docherty made Prime Minister!"

TARTAN TEASERS

How much do you know about Rod? Here are twenty questions for you to test yourself on, covering most sides of the tartan throated singer's career. If you get more than fifteen correct, you most certainly are a Stewart fan. Less than ten? There's nothing wrong with that—perhaps you just aren't very good at quizzes!

1. *Where was Rod born?*
2. *Do you know his parents' christian names?*
3. *What was the first group Rod worked with called?*
4. *What was the title of his first solo record?*
5. *In which year did Rod join the Faces?*
6. *What was the first album he recorded with them?*
7. *Can you name Rod's first solo album?*
8. *Rod once had a number one single and a number one LP at the same time on both sides of the Atlantic. Can you name them?*
9. *What was the line-up of the Faces (below) when Rod joined them?*

10. *Who is Rod's football hero (below)?*

11. *Which band was Jim Cregan with before he joined Rod?*

12. *Back in the sixties, Rod played the harmonica on a girl singer's big hit. Can you name her (pictured below) and the record?*

13. *With which month of the year would you associate Rod's first number one single?*

14. *Can you complete this album title? A – – – – – on – – – – – – –*

15. *Which ocean did Rod once cross on record?*

16. *Who (pictured right) was Rod's earliest musical influence?*

17. *Which sporting personality would Rod like to see made Prime Minister?*

18. *Rod often sings this one, but can you solve the anagram?*
LYNN
IDILY
ACCIDENT

19. *What is Rod's present record label?*

20. *Lastly, what was the first Rod Stewart single to be released under this label?*

ANSWERS

1. Highgate, North London; 2. Robert and Elsie; 3. Jimmy Powell's Five Dimensions; 4. *Good Morning Little School-girl*; **5. 1969; 6.** *First Step*; **7.** *An Old Raincoat Will Never Let You Down*; **8.** *Maggie May* **and** *Every Picture Tells a Story*; **9. Ronnie Lane, Ian MacLagan, Kenny Jones, Ron Wood and Rod himself; 10. Denis Law; 11. Steve Harley's Cockney Rebel; 12. Millie's** *My Boy Lollipop*; **13. (Maggie) May; 14.** *A Night on the Town*; **15. Atlantic (Crossing); 16. Al Jolson; 17. Tommy Docherty; 18.** *Cindy Incidentally*; **19. Riva; 20.** *Tonight's the Night.*

THE ROD STEWART GROUP

One of the more persistent guessing games in the music business began when Rod Stewart left the Faces in 1975. Speculation about who would win the highly-prized slots in a new Stewart band ran rampant through the course of Rod's work on his solo album A Night On The Town.

Finally, in August of '76, after a rigorous bout of auditioning, six faces emerged. Some of them were familiar; some relative newcomers. Half are American; half can claim Commonwealth status. They come

The Rod Stewart Group are, left to right: Jim Cregan, Billy Peek, Rod, Carmine Appice, Philip Chen, Gary Grainger and John Jarvis.

from diverse backgrounds as far afield as classical and reggae, but together they make some *rock band.*

CARMINE APPICE

Carmine (pronounced CAR-mine) has been breaking new ground in drumming for nigh on one decade. Born in New York City, he graduated at nineteen from the wedding and bar mitzvah circuit to a group called the Pigeons, who eventually became Vanilla Fudge. With their high-powered harmonies and expansive sound, Fudge were one of the first pop groups to take on the so-called 'progressive' look. Appice's heavy-handed, innovative drumming helped lift the pop drummer out of the background role and into the performing spotlight.

He's known Stewart since 1968 and, in fact, almost joined the Jeff Beck Band when Rod was the featured vocalist.

JOHN JARVIS

John Jarvis is the youngest member of the band. His determined rise to session prominence has been nothing short of meteoric. From Pasadena, California, he was signed to a publishing company by the time he was fifteen. His big break came when Art Garfunkel, on a recent solo LP, used some songs written by a friend of his. Jarvis was asked to contribute keyboard work and has since played on albums for Ringo Starr, Leo Sayer and Stewart's *A Night On The Town.*

Incredibly, Rod Stewart's band is the first pro band John's ever been in. "I just never

found a band I liked," says Jarvis!

GARY GRAINGER

Gary Grainger was born in the Kilburn district of North London. Originally a drummer, he was won over to electric guitar by the guitar sound of the Shadows and Buddy Holly. He is late of the hard-working English outfit called Strider, which he joined in 1973.

Grainger attracted the attention of Stewart when Strider accompanied the Faces on a '75 European tour. Apparently, the impression was a lasting one. When it came time for an audition for the new band, he was summoned and quickly selected. Of the three guitarists in the band, says Gary: "We all have different ways of playing. I'm more the raunchy kind of player, which seems to blend well with Jim and Billy."

BILLY PEEK

Since he's spent most of his career burning up fretboards alongside Chuck Berry, it's not surprising that Billy Peek has been dubbed 'the rock 'n' roller' of the Stewart band. A Berry protégé, Peek developed, in his years of biting back-up with Berry, a chomping old-school style of rockin' very compatible with Stewart's tastes.

Born in St. Louis, Peek was introduced to music by his father's guitar playing. "If it wasn't for him I never would've got started at all." After making the rounds of the club circuit in St. Louis, Peek joined Berry in 1969. The association led to five albums, a European tour and heavy road-work in North America. Peek can state unequivocably from the experience that, "when it comes to rock and roll, I can play it".

JIM CREGAN

Though he was born in the pastoral county of Somerset, Jim Cregan spent most of his life in London, cutting a wide berth through the English music scene. His early credits involve stints with the post-Rory Gallagher jazz-rock group Taste, and the influential Family, the progressive conglomerate with whom he played bass. Of his past work, he considers his work with English jazz singer Linda Lewis as, "musically providing me with the most enjoyment because it was the most demanding".

His recent notoriety has come from his role in Cockney Rebel, featuring the inimitable Steve Harley. Cregan logged two years in Rebel and found considerable artistic freedom within the group, but when the Stewart offer appeared, "it was too good to resist".

A finesse player, Cregan complements the rougher edge of his fellow guitarists in Stewart's band. "Billy Peek is untouchable on the rock and roll tunes," he maintains, "while the rest of the work is between Gary and myself. We do a lot of harmony work together." Cregan is delighted with the level of musicianship in the

band, and that assured, concerns himself now with getting the Americans in the group to speak proper English.

PHILIP CHEN

Bringing to the band yet another musical environment is bassist Philip Chen. While it may finally now be a household name, reggae was unheard of outside the Caribbean when Chen, from Kingston, Jamaica, hit London in the mid-60s with Jimmy James and the Vagabonds. Chen came to England with the Vagabonds as a spare guitarist. His on-again-off-again membership status in the band often depended on how much room there was on stage at the Vagabonds' cramped pub venues. If there was room, Chen played. He became an official member when he replaced the band's departed bassist. After taking up the four-stringed cause, he went on to pioneer reggae with the group for five years until he left in 1970 to pursue studio work.

Chen's studio credits have piled up furiously since then, including work with Jeff Beck, Donovan, Jimmy Witherspoon, Toots and the Maytals, Pete Townsend (the *Tommy* soundtrack), Johnny Nash and Jim Capaldi.

"I figured I had covered all the session business," says Chen, explaining his decision to join Stewart's band. "Studio work wasn't much of a challenge anymore and I always liked Rod's singing, so it was natural." As surely and tirelessly as he dedicated himself to session playing, Chen now hurls all his energies into the Stewart project. "I'm not interested in any more session work," he contends. "I'm gonna devote all my time to Rod."

TARTAN

A ROD STEWA

By its very nature, a discography can only be as complete as the last record issued. This track record of Rod Stewart's recording career takes us up to the end of 1976, and includes recordings made with the Hoochie Coochie Men, Shotgun Express, the Jeff Beck Group and the Faces, as well as solo releases.

SINGLES

The Hoochie Coochie Men
1964 *Up Above My Head* (b side)

Shotgun Express
1966 *I Could Feel the Whole World Turn Around* . . . Columbia

The Jeff Beck Group
1968 *I've Been Drinking* (b side) . . . EMI/Columbia
1969 *Plynth (Water Down the Drain)* . . . Columbia

Faces
1970 *Flying* . . . Warner Bros
1971 *Rear Wheel Skid* . . . Warner Bros
1971 *Stay With Me* . . . Warner Bros
1973 *Cindy Incidentally* . . . Warner Bros
1973 *Dishevelment Blues* . . . (given away free with NME)
1973 *Pool Hall Richard* . . . Warner Bros
1974 *Cindy Incidentally/Stay With Me/Pool Hall Richard* . . . Warner Bros EP
1974 *You Can Make Me Dance, Sing or Anything* . . . Warner Bros

Rod Stewart and the Faces
1976 *Cindy Incidentally/Stay With Me/You Can Make Me Dance, Sing or Anything* . . . Warner Bros Maxi Single

Rod Stewart
1964 *Good Morning Little Schoolgirl* . . . Decca
1965 *The Day Will Come* . . . Columbia
1965 *Shake* . . . Columbia
1966 *Little Miss Understood* (with Mike D'Abo) . . . Immediate

TRACKS
DISCOGRAPHY

1970 *It's All Over Now/Jo's Lament* . . . Vertigo
1971 *Maggie May/Reason to Believe* . . . Mercury
1972 *You Wear it Well/Lost Paraguayos* . . . Mercury
1972 *In a Broken Dream/Boogie Woogie Joe* . . . Young Blood
(This single, originally issued in 1971, was recorded under the name of Python Lee Jackson)
1972 *What Made Milwaukee Famous/Angel* . . . Mercury
1973 *Oh No Not My Baby* . . . Mercury
1974 *Farewell/Bring it on Home to Me/You Send Me* . . . Mercury
1975 *Sailing* . . . Warner Bros
1976 *Tonight's the Night* . . . Riva
1976 *This Old Heart of Mine* . . . Riva
1976 *The Killing of Georgie* . . . Riva
1976 *Get Back* . . . Riva
1977 *Don't Want To Talk About It/First Cut Is The Deepest* . . . Riva

ALBUMS

With the Jeff Beck Group
1968 *Truth* . . . EMI/Columbia
1969 *Beck-Ola* . . . EMI/Columbia

With the Faces
1970 *First Step* . . . Warner Bros
1971 *Long Player* . . . Warner Bros
1971 *A Nod's as Good as a Wink to a Blind Horse* . . . Warner Bros
1973 *Ooh La La* . . . Warner Bros
1973 *Coast to Coast Overture and Beginners* . . . Warner Bros
1977 *Best of The Faces* . . . Riva

Solo
1970 *An Old Raincoat Will Never Let You Down* . . . Vertigo
1970 *Gasoline Alley* . . . Vertigo
1971 *Every Picture Tells a Story* . . . Mercury
1972 *Never a Dull Moment* . . . Mercury
1973 *Sing it Again, Rod* . . . Mercury
1974 *Smiler* . . . Mercury
1975 *Atlantic Crossing* . . . Warner Bros
1976 *A Night on the Town* . . . Riva